"Happy Birthday"

The Story of the World's Most Popular Song

"Happy Birthday"

The Story of the World's Most Popular Song

By Nancy Kelly Allen

Illustrated by Gary Undercuffler

PELICAN PUBLISHING COMPANY

GRETNA 2010

For Sterling and Sherry

*The word "Pelican" and the depiction of a pelican
are trademarks of Pelican Publishing Company, Inc.,
and are registered in the U.S. Patent and Trademark Office.*

Library of Congress Cataloging-in-Publication Data

Allen, Nancy Kelly, 1949-
  Happy birthday : the story of the world's most popular song / by Nancy Kelly Allen ;
illustrated by Gary Undercuffler.
    p. cm.
  ISBN 978-1-58980-675-7 (alk. paper)
  1. Hill, Mildred J., 1859-1916. Happy birthday to you—Juvenile literature. 2. Hill,
Patty Smith, 1868-1946—Juvenile literature. I. Undercuffler, Gary, ill. II. Title.
  ML3930.H56A45 2010
  782.42'158—dc22

2009030281

Photographs of the Hill sisters used as source material for the illustrations were
provided by the Association for Childhood Education International (ACEI).

Additional photographs of the Hill family and other historical information used as
source material for the illustrations were provided by the Filson Historical Society in
Louisville, Kentucky.

Printed in Singapore
Published by Pelican Publishing Company, Inc.
1000 Burmaster Street, Gretna, Louisiana 70053

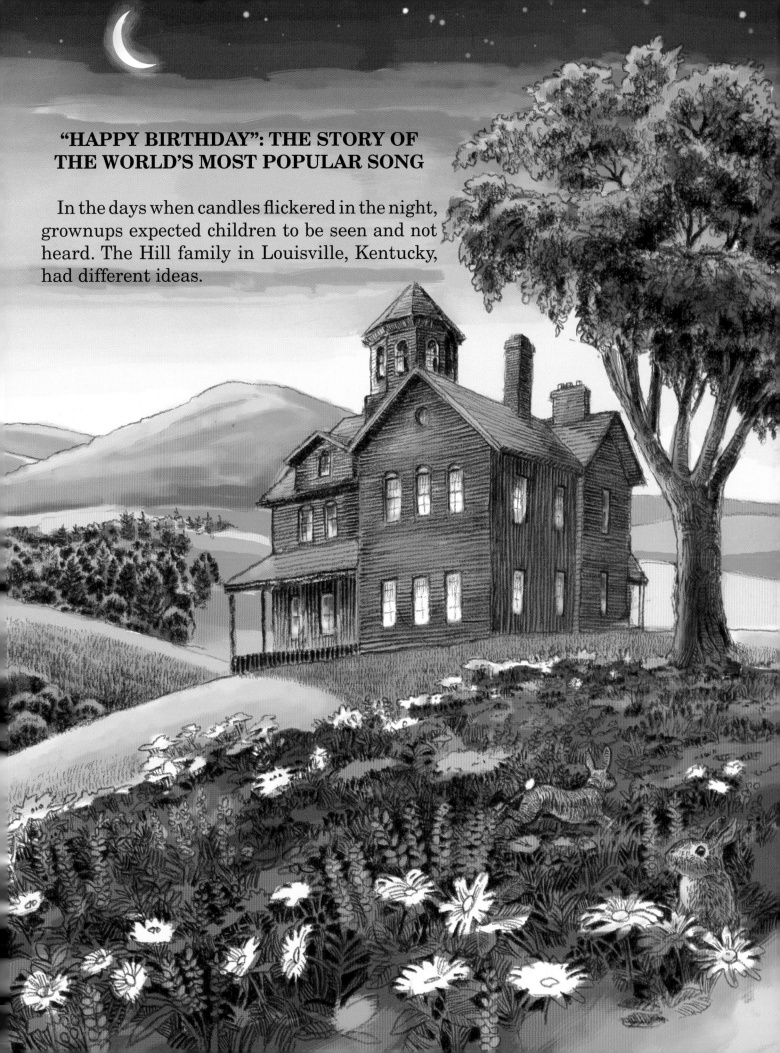

"HAPPY BIRTHDAY": THE STORY OF THE WORLD'S MOST POPULAR SONG

In the days when candles flickered in the night, grownups expected children to be seen and not heard. The Hill family in Louisville, Kentucky, had different ideas.

Martha, the mother, believed that children should speak up and laugh out as they learned. Her four daughters and two sons chased through the woods counting trees and studying leaves.

They built bridges, brick by brick, over tiny streams and traipsed back and forth. They connected barrels, end to end, and crawled through the dark tunnels. The adventuresome Hill children worked hard at playing.

William, the father, had other ideas about learning. He believed that girls, as well as boys, should get a college education so they could make a living for themselves.

To him, books fed the mind and music fed the soul, and nothing set feet to tapping and fingers a-snapping like a heaping helping of rhythm. William's idea of a good education included spending time with the piano and claiming it as a best friend.

Mildred, the oldest child, made the piano zing as she tickled the ivories with sassy tunes. Some say her talent came from learning to play as a young tot when her father taught her to fire up the keys with a song. Some say her talent was honed sharp as a razor by her music teachers, Calvin Cody and Adolph Weidig. Others say she had a natural talent, pure and sweet and clear. Everyone agreed, Mildred could pluck a melody out of thin air.

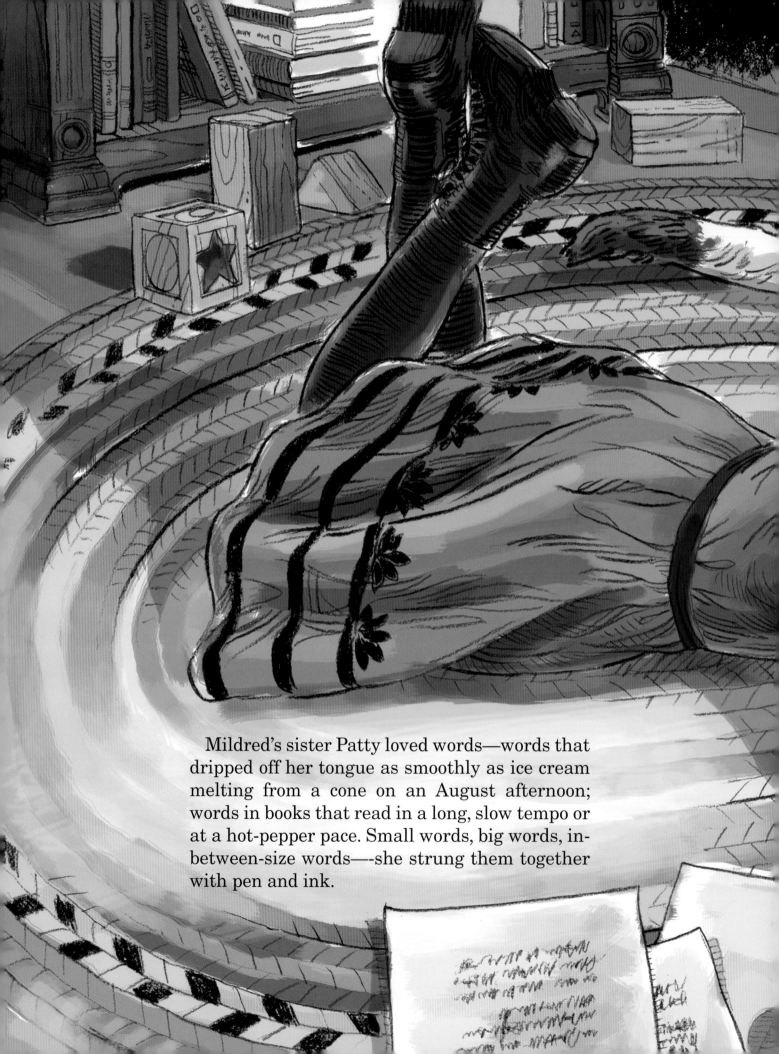

Mildred's sister Patty loved words—words that dripped off her tongue as smoothly as ice cream melting from a cone on an August afternoon; words in books that read in a long, slow tempo or at a hot-pepper pace. Small words, big words, in-between-size words—-she strung them together with pen and ink.

When Mildred finished high school, she set out for college. Patty soon followed and graduated in 1887. After college, they marched—*pit-a-pat tip-tap*—to the Louisville Experimental School, where Mildred taught kindergarten and Patty was the principal.

Like their mother, Mildred and Patty believed
that young children should enjoy learning through
play and games.

And like their father, they believed that music
was as important to education as words to a book.

Mildred loved the rhythms that surrounded her at school—the *foosh-foosh* of flicking pages, the *thump-thud-thump-thud clackety-clack* of the horses and buggies passing by on the street, the *ding-a-ding-a-ding-a-ding* of the bell she held in her hand.

The ringing signaled a new day of games and music and flicking pages in the kindergarten class she taught.

Patty enjoyed talking with the students and
listening to their ideas. She especially enjoyed
watching them construct buildings and bridges
with the "Patty Hill blocks" she invented.

Music jingled the air as Mildred dreamed up fun, bubbly tunes on the piano. Patty tapped her pen to the beat as she lined up words, one by one. Together, the sisters mixed the music with the words, song after song.

One day, the sisters wrote a song to sing to kindergarten students, to greet the day. They mixed and matched the words and music until they agreed on a little ditty: "Good Morning to All."

The next day, Mildred plunked down the tune on her piano and belted out "Good Morning to All" to her kindergarten students. She watched the children wiggle to the beat. When she sang the last note, a sizzle of applause heated the classroom.

Mildred's students knew a good thing when they heard it, so they asked her to sing "Good Morning to All" each day. Mildred played with vim and vigor and polished her performance 'til it spit-shined.

Mildred and Patty had another good idea. They collected the songs they had written for children and in 1893 published them in a book, *Song Stories for the Kindergarten*. Before long, "Good Morning to All" spread like sweet butter on a hot pancake. Other teachers across Louisville began singing it to their students. Then other teachers across the nation latched on to the tune.

One day at a birthday party, a string of words flashed as bright as shooting stars through Patty's mind. The words stuck, and the more Patty thought about them, the brighter the idea seemed. Then and there, she changed the words to "Good Morning to All" and sang the new ditty for the first time ever.

The catchy song was easy to remember, and people began singing it at parties. The song found its way out of Louisville, across the nation, and around the world.

Actors on television and in movies and plays have warbled the tune. Patty's brilliant idea has brightened the days of kings, presidents, and families the world over. It was the first song performed in outer space, crooned by the Apollo IX astronauts in 1969.